LIFE LINES

LIFE LINES

QUOTATIONS FROM THE WORK OF

EUGEN ROSENSTOCK-HUESSY

EDITED BY

CLINTON C. GARDNER

ARGO BOOKS

NORWICH, VERMONT

Wipf and Stock Publishers
199 W 8th Ave, Suite 3
Eugene, OR 97401

Life Lines
Quotations from the Work of
Eugen Rosenstock-Huessy
By Rosenstock-Huessy, Eugen
and Gardiner, Clinton C.

ISBN 13: 978-1-62032-454-7
Publication date 1/28/2013
Previously published by Argo
Books, 1988

Distributed and managed by
Wipf and Stock Publishers.
For all orders and inquiries
please contact us at:
http://www.wipfandstock.com
info@wipfandstock.com
orders@wipfandstock.com

Norwich, Ver-
be obtained
n Europe copies
erstraat 20,

ublication Data

73.

Gardner, Clinton

88-19392

Cover design by Kate Siepmann

Contents

Editor's Preface

I remember being told, as a child, that one should not mark up one's books. Fortunately, I avoided this advice, or this book might not have come about. Since the 1940s, when I studied with Eugen Rosenstock-Huessy at Dartmouth, I've been underlining his books with the zeal of a miner discovering nuggets. As I found kindred "miners," we began to discuss the idea of an anthology or collection of aphorisms.

Two of my friends, in fact, produced such books. Bruce Boston, in the early 1970s, prepared a sparkling collection of Rosenstock-Huessy aphorisms he called *Winepressings*—and almost found a publisher. Al Dahma, in 1973, self-published a comprehensive collection of quotations as *An Anthology of the Works of Eugen Rosenstock-Huessy.*

To produce *this* book I started by making selections from those two volumes. Since a selection of short, aphoristic quotations was my goal, it soon became apparent that Bruce Boston's *Winepressings* would become my largest source. I and the reader owe him special thanks for this.

I then invited other Rosenstock-Huessy students to send me their favorite quotations. Before long I had a pool of several thousand contributions. By far the most came from two books: *The Christian Future* and *Out of Revolution*. A large group was sent by George Morgan, with especially rich selections from German works. Other contributors included: Loren House, Raymond Huessy, William Martin, Lise van der Molen, and Lauren Pfister.

As contributions arrived, I compared them with the several thousand that I had selected over the years. Whenever I found quotations that matched mine, or when two others had selected the same quote, I flagged them as priorities for inclusion. Considerably more than half the quotations from *The Christian Future* and *Out of Revolution* fell into that category. Thus, the selection here represents a certain degree of "consensus" among Rosenstock-Huessy readers.

But it wasn't only Rosenstock-Huessy's books that yielded "nuggets." In 1972 I copied most of Rosenstock-Huessy's taped lectures so that Argo Books could sell them. In the course of listening to several hundred hours of tapes, I noted down more than several hundred eloquent and compact passages. Currently Mark and Francie Huessy are recopying and transcribing the taped lectures. They have been good enough to send many passages which I have included here.

Quotation sources are indicated in this book by letter codes after each quotation. Generally, books have two-letter codes, while articles and tapes have three-letter codes. Page numbers are provided for books. The bibliography lists all books, articles and tapes with their codes.

* * *

I and my collaborators on this book hope that *Life Lines* will prove to be an attractive introduction to our teacher. Unfortunately, there is not one particular Rosenstock-Huessy book which provides a ready introduction to the rest of his work. Perhaps *The Christian Future* or *The Multiformity of Man* come closest. But something even simpler, such as *Life Lines,* may help. Our children and grandchildren are probably even more suspicious of philosophy and theology than we were. This book is conceived for them, for the generations born after the Second World War.

Those of us who studied with Rosenstock-Huessy know that he was *very* suspicious of philosophy and theology. Yet those were the fields in which he tended to be categorized. He expressed his resistance to such categorization as follows:

> "I have survived decades of study and teaching in scholastic and academic sciences. Every one of their venerable scholars mistook me for the intellectual type which he most despised. The atheist wanted me to disappear into Divinity, the theologians into sociology, the sociologists into history, the historians into journalism, the

> journalists into metaphysics, the philosophers into law, and—need I say it?—the lawyers into hell, which as a member of our present world, I never had left." (*Out of Revolution,* p. 758.)

It is as "members of this present world" that Rosenstock-Huessy wants to address his listeners. He constantly challenges traditional categories of thought—in order to reach us where we really live and work. As early as 1919 he more or less abandoned the regular academic track when he went to work in the Daimler-Benz factory. And, while he subsequently taught in many universities, he was usually at odds with the universe of academic discourse. At least *that* will become clear to the reader of this book! His remarkable biography, in summary form, is provided as our last section, along with his picture.

While Rosenstock-Huessy was generally at odds with academe, he was often honored by it. Dartmouth had no professor with as many advanced degrees. As you'll note in our bibliography, he published 32 major books, again as many booklets, and 388 articles.

Now, as of 1988, there are three books which provide general introductions to Rosenstock-Huessy's work: George Morgan's *Speech and Society;* my own *Letters to The Third Millennium;* and Harold Stahmer's *"Speak That I May See Thee!"* (see bibliography page 79).

This book is being published in August 1988 in connection with a conference at Dartmouth

College marking the centennial of Rosenstock-Huessy's birth. This is actually the third international conference on his work. The first was held at the University of Waterloo in.Canada in 1982. (That conference's papers are published in *Eugen Rosenstock-Huessy: Studies in His Life and Thought,* edited by M. Darrol Bryant and Hans R. Huessy.) The second conference was held at The Free University in Berlin in 1985. All three conferences have produced papers which will certainly expand the circles in which Rosenstock-Huessy is appreciated. Yet somehow, I think, his students and friends hope for a more public and inter-generational appreciation. It is toward that wider circle "beyond conferences" that this book is addressed.

Rosenstock-Huessy suggested that new thought took at least three generations to establish. I hope that the words in this book will inspire my grandchildren's generation as they did those of us who studied with him at Dartmouth. If these words continue to echo now, perhaps by the third millennium they will "break loose" to serve the universities, churches and new institutions for which they were intended. Then they could help establish that "new thinking" which Rosenstock-Huessy and his friend Franz Rosenzweig felt would be needed to enter a new time, the time of "the Great Society," the time of a planet at peace with itself.

Clinton C. Gardner

I. The Individual & Society

ART

Art is an imitation of the lovable—it plays with the lovable. The strong is not lovable and the frail is. Art is love at play. - CRO

To be artistic means to be able to see the world today as though it never had existed before. The artist is that eye and ear and taste of first wonder at the dawn of creation. Art is the dream of humanity's spring, eternally young, eternally surprising. - ARC 5

BELIEF

He who believes in nothing still needs a girl to believe in him. - SOII 744

To believe means to recognize that we must wait until the veil shall be removed. Unbelief prematurely unveils itself. - VAU

CLASS WAR

The Class-War between Capital and Labor is as true and untrue as the sex-war between man and wife, the age-war between young and old, the border war between neighboring groups. - OR 79

COMMITMENT

The heart of man either falls in love with somebody or something, or it falls ill. It can never go unoccupied. - OR 4

Anything a man is truly willing to die for is stronger than anything people merely live on. - OR 4

CREATING

Conceiving a work is at the same time a change in quality of our own nature. You cannot create except by being recreated yourself. - ARC 13

CREATION

Anybody who has proposed to a girl knows that he is a different person after—on the day after she has said "Yes." So he knows what creation out of nothingness is. - COR

Just as there are moose, and buffaloes, and doves, and eagles, there are ways of life that have the same honor of being created. That is, man, when he had the right spirit—the Church calls this the Holy Spirit—has always continued creation. - UH4

Not revelation, creation makes us members of mankind, but so that any member is representing the whole kind, and still has a partial function too. - CLF 38

CREATIVITY

The highest life, the engendering, conceiving, inspired, devoted, in short all creative life, needs the times of night and day, darkness and brightness in succession. - SOII 43

THE CROSS OF REALITY

Man's life, social as well as individual, is lived at a crossroads between four "fronts": backward, forward, inward, and outward. It is obviously fatal to fail on any front....Integration, living a complete and full life, is accordingly not some smooth "adjustment" we can hope to achieve once for all, as popular psychology imagines: it is rather a constant achievement in the teeth of forces which tear us apart on the Cross of Reality. - CF 168

CURSING

The pious hatred of the Puritans against curses by now has made man impotent to bless. Nobody has the power to bless or be blessed who has lost the vigor to curse. Our society is so polite that it cannot curse social evils and prefers to blaspheme God instead. - CF 24

DIVORCE

The simple fact that people assume divorce is possible wrecks many marriages. - OS 122

DRAMA

Drama is the highest art because it represents

the conflict between the hero's experience of the next time and the present time. - CRO

ECONOMIC CHANGE

Every change in the rhythm of life hurts. The pains of rhythm-change embarrass us. It must therefore be consciously rehearsed to become bearable. The most modern entrepreneur and the most remote Brazilian villagers share these growing pains of incessant rhythm-change. - FEW 39

ELDERS

The secret of eldership lies in the fact that an old man is through with his own life but not at all through with life....It is the expectation of one day becoming elders that should carry us through the full cycle of our own lives....Without elders, who embody the secret of survival, the group itself is lost. - IA 104

ETHICS

True action is not responsible to so-called ethics. A vital issue rises above the known good and evil because it leads into the unknown. The results of all our crucial actions are hidden from us. - OR 720

FACTS & EVENTS

The word "event" is the backbone of all history, and the word "fact" is the backbone of all science. Facts are repetitive; events are unique. - UH4

FREE ENTERPRISE

As you know our corporations today thrive on the fiction of free enterprise and small business. I mean big business has even a small business committee in the Congress to prevent small business from existing. - UH6

GOOD & EVIL

Evil increases automatically. Inertia, laziness, cowardice, death are self-multiplying. Good "is" not, except by propagation; it is not in any man, but originates only between. - IA 26

GRACE

As soon as we place grace where it belongs, in the center of life, as its inspiration, life ceases to be arbitrary or accidental or casual and boring. - CLF 48

HEROES

A hero is only a hero if his grandchildren still mention him. You cannot be a hero to your own generation. - UH4

HOPE & FAITH

Man is equipped with two great forces—hope and faith—compared to which his intelligence is a minor matter. It is a harlot, a tool. If you have faith, you will live forward in spite of disappointment. If you have hope, you will let nothing die that once proved worthwhile. - UH4

HUMAN NATURE

Any real man behaves in the volcanic hours of his own life as people behaved during revolutions. Those hours are extreme and terrible, yet they tell us more about the unity of human nature than soft days of peace from which behaviorists are apt to derive their political concepts. - OR 708

THE IMPOSSIBLE

The necessary is always the one thing that has been deemed to be impossible until it was done. - CRO

INDUSTRY

The man who works in industry is a peculiar human being because his sense for time and timing is conditioned by the dilemma of management. The worker is a man who must never forget that a boom town may become a ghost town over night and that his skill may be replaced by a robot in the afternoon. - MM 5

INHERITING & BEQUEATHING

People who have neither inherited something nor bequeathed something worth inheriting vanish without a trace. - ER 513

LIBERALS & CONSERVATIVES

Anybody in our midst who boasts that he is a liberal or a conservative obviously cannot count up to three....Nobody can be anything but a liberal-conservative or a progressive-reactionary. - PEM 24

LIBERATING OURSELVES

All our lives we must remain able to drop everything when it becomes too stupid or unjust: all submission, all the power of the soul, belongs at the point in life where we liberate ourselves anew. - PSI 329

LIFE

The full life has a beat. - CF 208

To live means to change allegiances at the right moment. - UH4

In life the act precedes the fact, verbs which proclaim action precede nouns which register the result. - AG 20

Living is but one half of life, the repetitive and predictable part. The other half is the agonizing creation and the creative agony of dying and being born. - CF 57

We postulate as a condition of all life that it must turn itself against its own gravitation and be able to transform itself contrary to its own structures. - AG 66

LOVE

Whoever says, "I love," must either blush or he lies. - JN 33

Love is there to overcome death. - COR

Man has as much knowledge as he has invoked love, or evoked love, you can also say....Man can only know as many things as he can love. - COR

LOVE & SUFFERING

Love disarms; suffering overpowers. - PS 108

LOVERS

All those less in love owe secrecy to the lovers. - AG 50

THE MACHINE AGE

The Christian soldier of the future must wage war against the indifference and indolence, the coldness and barrenness of human relations in the machine age. - CF 27

MAN

Man is the resistance with which reality must reckon; he is the adversary of reality. - SOI 2

Any man who says he is "just" something has ceased to live. How can he know what he will be tomorrow? - CRO

Man is the up-hill animal of creation. - CLF 50

MANAGERS

A manager who would think of himself as a Leader would be a Fascist. - MM 4

MANKIND

We already know that the solidarity of the human race is the meaning of mankind, that here is an animal that, compared to the elephant, or compared to the ant, is destined to be one over the whole globe. - UH6

MARRIAGE

We are so dull that we rarely realize how much history lies hidden in marriage and how one word spoken by the bride makes all the difference between cattle-raising and a nation's good breeding. - OR 9

You cannot take a calculated risk when you marry. If it is a calculation, then it is no risk. If it is a risk, then it is unlimited. Risk is a secular term for faith; faith is the act which you do because you have to do it. - CRO

In any true fellowship, as in marriage, the relationship of different points of view is not handled controversially....The logic of an argument between husband and wife consists in the husband defending the wife's interest, and the wife, that of the husband. - PEM 23

When a man stays married and doesn't run off with another wife—which would be very tempting in itself to do, if he only considered his own existence—he does this for the next generation. The sacrament of marriage has nothing to do with the relation of one man and one woman, but it is absolutely necessary if you want to make the next generation realize the peace that can exist between two sexes. - UH6

It is much more difficult to believe in marriage than to believe in God. - OS 26

MEN & WOMEN

Only that is important to which both men and women contribute. - OS 87

MODESTY

Without modesty there is no growth of the soul. If the soul were an It or an I, thing or god, it would not need modesty. But a human soul, as Thou, conceals itself. - SMI 778

OBEYING

The child which is not made to obey is denied the power ever to command. - IA 73

ORGANIZATION

The hallmark of dead things is that they can be organized. - PSI 331

ORIGINALITY

Any original thinker knows that he has to jump; later you can build bridges. - CRO

PARTNERSHIP

In a contract I try to get as much as possible and to remain as unchanged as possible. In any partnership I throw in my lot today without knowing where I will be tomorrow. - MM 55

PROGRESS

The future does not stay open automatically; it has to be reopened by your own inward death and renewal. Not steady movement in one direction but continual redirection, breaking through old ruts, is the formula for progress. - CF 83

SACRIFICE

The problem of your and my life is that your death can be the beginning of a glorious life in somebody else....Every sacrifice, every renunciation you make, can be called your death and another person's birth. We beget all the time, with every renunciation. - UH6

Anything a man is ready to die for is stronger than anything people merely live on. - OR 542

SEEING

First rate experiences are never gained through the eye . - SOII 33

SEX

Sexuality throws no light upon love, but only through love can we learn to understand sexuality. - VAU

SOCIALISM

Socialism is the dictatorship of theory over the proletariat. - INV 21

SPECIALIZATION

Those who are diffused into areas of competence reach everybody, but not into a single soul. - AG 41

SUBURBIA

Suburban life is unreal because it shuns pain and conflict. - CF 12

SUCCESS

By taking it for granted that success is the only desire of man, we deprive ourselves of the means to study the laws of the good life. - CLF 72

SUPERSTITION

You are surrounded by witchcraft and sorcerers. I assure you, never has a country been so benighted in the dark ages. Your advertisers, your psychoanalysts, your pacifists—they all have wrapped you into a shroud of superstition. - UH6

II. Time

DEATH

The most important fact that we know of, every individual's physical death, is not a fact of the past or of the present but of the future. - CLF 13

The word "future" attains its full meaning only when we assume and recognize the possibility of death between now and then. - AG 126

THE DIMENSIONS OF TIME

To reestablish the elementary fact that the human mind cannot think except in the three dimensions of time, is one of the most burning scientific needs of our age. - CLF 1

EXCITEMENT

Man excited always experiences himself in time and not in space, for he is excited when he says something unheard of before. - AG 26

FAITH IN THE FUTURE

Nobody in this country today has faith in the year 2200, at least not officially. If you read the editorials, you will see that they all believe that by then we shall have had a Third World War, and the whole world will have gone up in flames. Funny thing. Formerly, only the Christians believed in the end of the world, but today Christians are the only people who think that the world will still have a future, while all the agnostics believe in the end of the world, and all the atheists believe that nothing can prevent the self-destruction of the human race. - UH4

Faith, properly speaking, is never a belief in things of the past, but in the future. - SR 12

FUTURE

Men create future when they are more than doubtful about the stability of society as it is, and feel that the end of the world is ever imminent. - CF 80

FUTURE, PRESENT, PAST

What is the future? It is that for which it is right to sacrifice the present. - UH4

One long forgotten truth is re-established: that mankind's future and mankind's past both precede its present tense logically. - CLF 15

FUTURE & PROGRESS

Progress and future are indeed inseparable, but the order of their dependence is just the reverse. Precisely because Christianity creates future, progress is the gift of the Christian Era. - CF 75

GAINING TIME

To gain time, and to learn how to regain time, is the content of mankind's story of earth. It is the easiest thing in the world to work all the time, compared to the incredible difficulty of spending one hour or one day of rest in a proper way. - OR 14

GOOD & EVIL

The idealist who thinks anything can be good outside of time and space only makes a fool of himself. Timeliness is everything. Reality is "good" when it proceeds timely; it is bad when too late or too early. "Good" and "evil" themselves, in their deepest sense, mean ripeness and immaturity. - OR 720

Every generation has a new history, because it has a different future. - UH4

HOLIDAYS

The balance between workday and Sunday is an eternal demand of the human soul. - CF 212

A day introduced into the calendar or a day stricken out of the calendar, means a real change in the education and tradition of a nation. Mankind writes its own history long before the historians visit its battlefields; days, festivals, the order of meals, rest and vacations, together with religiously observed rituals and symbols, are sources of political history, though rarely used as such by the average political or economic historian. A holiday is a political creation and a political instrument. - OR 8

If you were to realize that the calendar is the great, honorable institution by which you are introduced into your humanity, you would not confuse the evenings off for plays with the great holidays of the human race. Easter is not a day for entertainment. - UH5

HOPE, FAITH, LOVE

Any Body of Time constitutes a fusion by which one's time in the form of future and another's time in the form of past are made accessible to each other by hope, faith, love. Without the mobilization of these three energies, the animal cannot become human, and the roving individual cannot ascend to the quality of reality, of being. - MMT 57

HUMANISM

Humanism accepted the division into past, present, and future as a natural fact which seemed to be inherent in the world outside of man. Humanism was mistaken. To divide time into past, future, and present is a creation of society. - MMT 57

IDLE TIME

Civilized people have more time than they have life: idle time gives birth to idle thoughts. - VAU

INHERITANCE

Our forefathers developed their notions about a common time from the laws of inheritance. The good old times were to be tied in, the present tied down, and the future tied on. The result was a small eternity, an aeon. - AG 116

MAN

Man is peculiarly a temporal being, ever but an exile and a pilgrim in the world of space. - IA 92

MOMENTS OF TIME

The concept of the generation is, in our language, nearly gone. It makes time rhythmic. Time is not the sequence of moments in history. It is incisive. The name-giving process which tries to get hold of your ancestor is incisive. There is no speech without holidays, without great events, without picking and choosing some moments of time to be lifted up out of the run of the mill of time. Man's history does not consist of the natural time of the scientist. It is not the sequence of 1000 years but the sequence of the beginning and the end, of instituted time. - UH4

NEW EVENTS

A great new event is more than an additional paragraph to be inserted in the next edition of a book. It rewrites history, it changes the past because it initiates a new future. Anyone who looks back on his own life knows how completely a new love, a new home, a new conviction, changes the aspect of his past. - OR 5

NIETZSCHE

"The future is the basis of our present evaluations," exclaimed the rediscoverer of the future and its logical function, Friedrich Nietzsche. - CLF 13

ORIENTATION

By refusing to acknowledge their indebtedness to the Christian era for one future, one time common to all men, scholars lose their orientation. Sciences do not give orientation; they presuppose it. The pillars of time are erected by lives lived, not by theories. - CF 86

OUR TIME

Man was created to belong to all times. To confine a person to his own time is to maim him. - AG 125

"Time," singular, is continuously created by the fusion of our individual, biological times—the time which can be called "our" time, which does not exist unless it is created. And we can create it only through the renunciation of every particular time. - AG 127

PRESENCE OF MIND

The present, whether it be an hour or a whole era, is not a natural fact but a constant social achievement. True presence of mind, the power to live in the fullness of time, has to be won arduously and preserved by perpetual vigilance. When a man rises above his future, which is the imminence of his death, and beyond his past, which is the reminiscence of his origins, he enters the present. - IA 91

THE PRESENT

All present is the intersection of at least two essentially disparate times to form an inexpressible common time. - AG 141

The present does not exist in nature. It is a gradual product of the three cardinal time-producing energies in society, and it has to be reproduced incessantly. The present may be lost. And then the world breaks apart into individuals who are neither young nor old but unteachable urchins and unimpressible martinets. - MMT 58

RIPENESS

The biography of a real human being includes a deeper secret than the fulfillment of one ideal or one philosophical system. Ripeness is everything. To take every step in life at the proper time is man's great personal mission. - MM 68

THE RUSSIANS

We say that causes produce results and that the past and the present produce the future. This is believed in all the schools of this country, not only here in America but in Europe too. Only the Russians know better. They say the future produces the present and abolishes the past, and that is true. - CRO

SPACES & TIMES

Architectonic spaces are repeatable spaces of time. Therefore spaces stand in the service of time. And it is the physicists, the powerful wizards of today, who stand the world of living on its head and would persuade us that space ranks before time, that time is a fifth or a senseless fourth dimension. It is much more the reverse. To the three dimensions of time, tomorrow, yesterday and today, the fourth dimension of space should be added. - GU 171

The truth is in the man who can equate and identify the times and spaces of his life. - SR 56

SURPRISES

Either time is a chain of endless surprises or it breaks down into a helpless conservatism. - OR 213

THEOLOGIANS & PHILOSOPHERS

Time withers in the hands of theologians, who are on good terms with eternity, and in the hands of the philosophers, who are obsessed by space. - AG 97

TIMES

Time is given to the real man (not to the abstraction called "physicist") as one in three: (1) the Times I enfold myself; (2) the Times which have preceded my consciousness; (3) the Times which follow after I am dead. - TIH 32

TIMING

Shame is the soul's garment against arbitrary and untimely knowledge, because timing is the condition in which alone the Eternal may be revealed. It takes time for a bride to know her love. It takes time for a nation to find her destiny. It takes time for the heart to know itself. The modern mind of man whispers instead: "It takes no time to know anything."- LTT 5

TRENDS

That which simply goes on from the past as a trend is not "future" in the full sense of the term. It simply travels on an extension visa from the past. In human history the break with the past is the condition of any future. The relation of any past and any future is never made by a trend, but always by a victory over trends. - CF 32

III. Speech

ACQUIRED CHARACTERISTICS

The West-East controversy with Lysenko about the acquisition of new characteristics is a question perversely put. Of course we incessantly acquire new characteristics and transmit them. That is the meaning of our history. Language transfers acquired characteristics. - SMI 303

ADVICE

Why is advice unasked for never given successfully? Because it has no power to unlock the recipient's ear. - SR 106

BEING TRANSFORMED

Whoever says something without being transformed by it himself does not speak the truth. - AG 84

BELIEF

Whoever speaks believes in the unity of mankind. And he believes that the unity of mankind is not produced by physical or political or economic or racial reasons but by our faith in speech. - SR 184

CARTESIAN BLINDNESS

To be called by his true name is part of any listener's process of becoming his true self. This is part of the process of being fully born. The United States of America did not exist before they were called the United States of America. Cartesian blindness to this reality of names disfigures most investigations of psychologists, sociologists and historians, who do not know that they are paralyzed by their Cartesian origins. - IA 66

CHATTER

I only begin to speak when I submit myself to my own words—observe by comparison children, who do not do this. Up to this point everything is empty chatter. - AG 68

CHILDREN

Never will a child be at peace which has not meant the world to somebody and has been spoken to as though it were the only child on earth. - OS 110

COMING TO YOURSELF

The pearls of speech are the fruit of coming to yourself. But what does that foolish "coming to yourself" mean? Well, becoming indifferent to your status, your reputation, your appearance, your rank, your honor, or your rights. - PS 105

COMMANDS

What we find between people who trust one another in commands given and fulfilled is not a frame of reference but a field of correspondence. - OS 47

CONCEPTS

Vital names grow obsolete, concepts do not. Hence names nourish and concepts do not. - AG 58

DECLARING

All religions are convinced that we have to speak up in order to live the good life. This is hard to explain, but you can perhaps explain it by what you do when you are in love. You must declare your love....The declaration of one's faith is part of the faith itself, as a declaration of love is part of love itself, as the declaration of war is part of war itself. - COR

EVOLUTION

To speak means to participate in the evolutionary adventure of speaking humanity. - SR 63

EXPECTANCY

Nothing great in this world can be achieved without great expectation. The expectancy of the listeners is a condition for every communication. Only in response to the messianic expectancy of all peoples could the Messiah come. And only what fulfills a longing finds an enduring place in history. - AG 17

GENERATIONS

The living speech of a community results from the polarization of acts and thoughts; like the spark which crosses the dark gap between the positive and negative poles of electricity, speech is a flaming arc connecting different generations. - CF 229

GOD, WORLD, MAN

God, World and Man are vocative and not nominative forms. They are intersections at which our word, the names of love, and the concepts of our work should meet. They are provocations to our answers. - AG 57

GODLESSNESS

Only he who gives no credence to his own sentences is godless. - SOII 628

GRAMMAR

Grammar and logic free language from being at the mercy of the tone of voice. Grammar protects us against misunderstanding the sound of an uttered name; logic protects us against what we say having a double meaning. - VAU

HEARING

Seeing puts us in an outer space, even facing our neighbor. But hearing I share the common inner space of all voices. - SOII 58

HISTORY

In living language all particular sentences, songs, speeches, books, national languages, literatures are only detached tones of a monotheistic but polyphonic symphony. Our sentences have meaning only in the polyglot of the choruses of human history. - SMI 369

I & THOU

God can never communicate something to me as long as I think of myself as an *I*. God recognizes me only as a *thou*. - SMI 105

I am a *thou* for society long before I am an *I* to myself. - OS 90

The soul must be called "Thou" before she can ever reply "I," before she can ever speak of "us" and finally "it." Through the four figures, "Thou, I, We, It," the Word walks through us. The Word must call our name first. We must have listened and obeyed before we can think or command. - LTT 12

IMPERATIVES

An imperative ceases to work when we look beyond its completion. - OS 121

Imperatives, not astronomers, make men move in history. - OS 54

Grammatically speaking, there is no "I" in the imperative; there is a "thou" in every listener's heart. - OS 90

INVOCATION

Language has been only created for the purpose of invocation. And all languages are cooling-off processes, as in geology. What you see of language today is the cooling-off after thousands of years of heated speech. - COR

By invocation, we unite. It's a first step of mutually inheriting the earth. - COR

All human names empower you to become one day the invoked. If you say, "Father," you also say that, although you are a son now, you may one day have to be a father. - COR

Knowledge, itself, without invocation kills. And the Americans kill their own soul every day by knowing more than they can love. - COR

LIFE & DEATH

Language, because it is life, is subject to the law of life, that it originates from death; life means overcoming death. When we live we must change every moment in order to keep alive, we must breathe. When we breathe together we speak, we are inspired. It is thus a struggle of the common life against decay through death. - GU 119

LISTENERS

Every speaker needs a listener who believes that it is worthwhile to listen! - OS 101

NAMES

The name is the conqueror of death in the political sense. "In the name of" is always said by the middle generation, trying to bring the past into the future. - UH4

Names make me look at those named. For this reason academics has no teaching of names; it abstracts, and by this very act declares names to be a fiction. - AG 54

Whenever a name is found for a thing, whenever a thing is seized and held by a word, the world grows larger; when it is only described, men stay in their accustomed grooves. - OR 468

Names were the first forms of man's voicing his desire to learn where he stood in the universe. - COR

Names are the way of incorporation. Names are the way of incorporating ourselves into each other. The name which I give you reflects or jumps back, recoils on me, and in this very moment we create a bridge. - COR

The religion of a man rests on the names that induce him to act jointly with others. These names may pass away, but in their day they are mightier, more valid, and contribute more to history, than private relations to a pretty face or to blood kin. - SMI 569

We live out of the future into the past, and this life force, this calling, grants us our name. - SMI 76

NAMES & DEATH

To be named establishes one into a time sequence with at least two epochal and decisive breaks: the death of the person who named me and the death of myself, the career of a name which is meant to survive any physical destruction. - TIH 31

NAMING

Everyone knows of God whose soul out of love has had to call somebody by the right name and been permitted to recognize him in virtue of this act of love. - SOII 329

NATURE

"Nature" is the world minus speech. It is a misleading word, because voices call us into life first of all, and water, earth and wind may concern us only after membership in society and participation in language secure us roped fast above the abyss of nature. - SMI 43

POETRY

Poetry begins where ritual leaves off. It takes the state of mind created by ritual for granted. It does not make man wise; it treats him as being initiated. - ROP

A poem is one exhalation of the soul. - ROP

Poetry is often the form which a scientific truth takes a century before it can be proven. - AG 67

Poetry is for the period what the daily bread is for the day. Poetry does not embellish life, it leads it to its proper fulfillment. - ROP

POTENCY

We experience the world by our work. We experience God without work. We experience Him in will-lessness; we experience Him in suffering. We experience Him in the progenitive act of love, and the first form of our potency, our generative power, is not sensuality but the word wooing for love. - HW 80

PRAISE

Praise is not a luxury. It is not an addition but it is the first utterance of a human soul. - COR

SCIENCE

Speech is contrary to all science because in speaking everybody must say something different, whereas the aim of science is that all must say the same thing. - AG 77

SOCIETY

The circulation of articulated speech is the life blood of society. - SR 16

SPEECH & DEATH

Language is the victory over death. It is a defiance of merely sensuous existence. - UH4

SPEECH AS MIRACLE

Speech is nothing natural; it is a miracle. - AG 34

SPIRIT

All speech is the precipitation of the intensified respiration which we experience as members of a community, and which is called the Spirit. - SMI 573

THINKING

Thinking is nothing but a storage room for speech. - COR

TIME

Without speech man would have no time but merely be immersed in time. Animals are time's toys. Men conquered time when they began to speak. - IA 115

TIMES & SPACES

By speaking we create times and spaces. Language does not describe. It creates a now and then as well as a here and there. - SOI 158

THE UNIVERSE

Mankind covers the whole of space and the whole of time more and more, because language conquers more and more space and time, and the reunification of languages unifies this universe of ours perpetually. Language creates one unique being through the ages. - LAL 11

VOCATIVES

The vocative makes it clear that I, the speaker, am destined to be the spoken to. I need it. Every vocative is an attempt at transformation. - GU 138

WHISPERING

Whispering is unauthorized speech. The devil is any person who does not wish to be quoted, and so never attains the rank of a person. For a person accepts God's judgment over what he has said or done. Thus he can come to know the truth. The devil never receives this verdict because he whispers only, and never speaks truly or confidently. - JD 188

WORDS & DEEDS

But how did Doolittle and Lincoln acquire their reputations? Certainly not by using language as a set, but by impressing people with the unity of their words and their actions. They made us feel that by word and deed they served in the same name. Names are so sacred because they constitute the unity or conflict of words and deeds in human life. Hence names are priceless; words have their price. - CF 8

IV. Religion

ACTING ONCE FOR ALL

This is the criterion of what is human that has been laid down by Christianity: how a man can be eternal in the moment, how he can act once for all. - AK 108

ATHEISM

Classrooms are atheistic by establishment. They are God's concession to our curiosity. - SR 181

CHRIST

Man and wife are opposites, yes, the statesman and his nation are opposites, Christ and his church are opposites, and often Christ is on the side of martyrs suffering from his church. - MM 53

You are participating in the strange idea that God never created men. He created one man. And He tries to make you and me one man from the beginning of time to the end of time. That's Christianity, by and large. One man is the son of God, not many. Jesus is not at all as Jesus of

Nazareth the son of God, but as Christ. That is, the center point through which all previous men and all later men form this one man with which God has dealings. God has no dealings with you privately. - UH6

CHRISTIANITY

"Saving" Christianity is unnecessary, undesirable, impossible, because it is anti-Christian. Christianity says that he who tries to save his soul shall lose it. Our supreme need is not to save what we smugly presume to have, but to revive what we have almost lost. - CF 61

Yes, Christianity is bankrupt today. But not refuted. Christianity has repeatedly been bankrupt. When it goes bankrupt, it begins all over again; therein rests its real power. - CF 89

Christianity is essentially war in peace: it distributes the bloody sacrifices of the battlefront by an even but perpetual spread of sacrifices through the whole fabric of life. - CF 26

CHRISTIANITY & FUTURE

At the center of the Christian Creed is faith in death and resurrection. Christians believe in an end of the world, not only once, but again and again. This and this alone is the power which enables us to die to our old habits and ideals, get out of our old ruts, leave our dead selves behind and take the first step into a genuine future. That is why Christianity and future are synonymous. - CF 62

Christianity came into a world of divided loyalties—races, classes, tribes, nations, empires, all living to themselves alone. It did not simply erase these loyalties; that would have plunged men into nihilism and cancelled the previous work of creation, and Jesus came not to deny but to fulfill. Rather, by its gift of a real future, Christianity implanted in the very midst of men's loyalties a power which, reaching back from the end of time, drew them step by step into unity. - CF 62

Through its creation of future, Christianity has endowed man, individually and collectively, with the power of having a life history....In the cyclic, pagan view of history everything we do has happened before; nothing of permanent value is achieved; there is only change, without beginning or end. - CF 71

CHRISTIANITY'S UNIVERSALITY

The belief in universal inspiration, in a permanent guidance of the Saints and the Holy Ghost, is the outstanding difference between the historical adventure of Christianity and the natural religions. Inspiration is perpetually transforming humanity. - OR 178

THE CHURCH

The Church is the power of any generation to harvest the fruits of previous generations and to sow the seeds of future generations. And a marriage, for example, does this. And therefore it's called a sacrament in many churches, because it bestows on the children something they cannot give themselves. The Church is the residue of all the things that nature cannot give. - UH6

In every generation the same coincidence of God and man that started in Jesus is realized by those who keep together in One Spirit. That is the meaning of the Church as the Body of Christ. - CF 108

CHURCH & STATE

As the economic sphere ceases to be a realm of individual freedom, the State threatens to become an all-engulfing leviathan. In former days, Christendom achieved a unique liberty for men, unknown in other cultures, by maintaining the duality of Church and State: every earthly city had to admit at least one building in its midst which was not of national origin; men saw two worlds, one national and the other divine, when they moved from State House to Meeting House, and the choice between the two allegiances prevented their enslavement by either. - CF 39

CONQUERING DEATH

Christianity did not come into the world to teach anything. It is not a doctrine. It came, as you know, to reveal something: the connection of death and life. - UH6

God becomes known to us in all the powers which triumph over death, and from the earliest times men have called any such power divine. - CF 92

The climax in conquering death, and therefore in man's knowledge of God, was the crucifixion and resurrection of Christ. By him, at last, death was included as a positive factor within life and was thereby finally and completely overcome: death became the gateway to the future, to new life. - CF 93

If the Divine becomes known in our lives as the power of conquering death, it is something that can only happen to us in this or that particular moment of time; it is known as an event, never as an essence or a thing. And it can happen to us only in the midst of living, after death in some form—bereavement, nervous breakdown, loss of hopes—has come upon us. Hence Christianity has no God in the sense of Aristotle or Plato or a modern deist who frames a concept of Him as prime mover, world soul, or first cause. - CF 94

If you have no connection with some grand-parent of the spirit, you have no future beyond your own grave. - CIR

CREATION

You should not read the Bible as though it said, "God had created the Heaven and earth." [What] it really means is God creates Heaven and earth. - COR

THE DEVIL

The refinement of the devil seems to be just this, that he pretends to do "nothing." In fact, he annuls. - LTT 15

THE ECUMENICAL MOVEMENT

No "ecumenical movements" will save us, as they spring from the purely geographical vision. Christianity never moves in space but it conquers death through new joints in time. - GNF 15

FAITH

We call faith the undaunted acceptance of one's death and a future without oneself...not the simple undauntedness of youth. Full-fledged faith reaches into the future. - AG 147

FAITH, HOPE & LOVE

Without faith man is but a stub of himself, because the future remains closed to him. Without hope man is cut off from his roots in the past, for they have ceased to arouse new wishes in him. And without love his neighbor is but a natural object because he is incapable of embracing the living present in unison with his neighbor. Faith takes time forwards, hope takes time backwards, love embraces the mere object so that it may share its present. - AG 100

No man loves who is unable to find a new name for his love. No man hopes who does not behold some beautiful new thing in this world. No man believes who does not acclaim God in new names whenever he uses the old. - AG 147

FAITH & REASON

Now the political value or force of a religion is its endlessness. Politics, being a process of realization, must be driven by the force of some unlimited faith. Only the infinite can move the finite. There lies the fatal superiority of faith over reason. - OR 331

FAITH, RELIGION, THEOLOGY

There are three things. The soul has faith. The cultural institution has religion. But the mentally trained scholastic has theology. And they are three very different things indeed. - UH6

Theology is the enemy of faith and religion, and it's the most vital and poisonous enemy of religion and faith, because it thinks about these things. - UH6

GOD

God does not speak to us in words, he speaks in forms and creatures. - OR 191

To have revealed what is not God is the condition of all our understanding of God. - JD 181

The power who puts questions into our mouth and makes us answer them is our God....Of course God is not a school examiner. Man never gives his real answer in words; he gives himself. - OR 725

The God who beckons us from the end of time as the common destiny of man is an abomination to the pagan leader because this living God is not found in any past. - JD 182

The gods pass. When the individual realizes their passing, their unceasing change, he is converted to God—the living God who invites us to obey the *"unum necessarium,"* the one thing necessary and timely at every moment. - OR 727

GOD & SPEECH

We name our gods, but God makes us speak. - SMI 53

Nobody can look at God as an object. God looks at us and has looked at us before we open our eyes or our mouths. He is the power which makes us speak. He puts words of life on our lips. - CF 94

It is quite unimportant whether a man knows that he believes in God or not. The power to speak is God because it unites me with all men and makes us judges of the whole world. - SR 184

God simply is the power to speak the truth, with such consecutive results that that which is said also happens. Everybody who speaks believes in God because he speaks. No declaration of faith is necessary. No religion. - SR 181

GOD'S MIND

Scientists often look down on people who speak

of being in the face of God, or of the fingers of God, as being hopelessly superstitious, while they speak of God's mind themselves. But the mind of God is as much a metaphor as his elbow. - SMII 228

GOD THE SON

The Son restores the proper order between words spoken and lives lived. Words should be orders given, promises made. Lives should be orders carried out and promises fulfilled. This had been the essential aim of all speech and ritual since man spoke. - FL 125

GENERATIONS

Why is God so inexhaustibly original? Because he rethinks the world for every generation of his children. - CF 231

GOLF CLUB CHRISTIANS

Hitler is not an accident. Hitler is the answer to liberal parents who wouldn't speak to their children about God, or about the future, or about anything. They were golf club Christians or country club Christians. - UH6

IDEALISM

Christianity has always felt closer to zoologists than to idealists. Christianity is not idealism. - UH6

IMMORTALITY

Man is not immortal in the ridiculous sense of the Greeks, that man just didn't die, and the mind went on forever. This immortality doesn't exist. But life can die in me and rise in you. That's all we have. - UH6

THE INVISIBLE

God is invisible. Hence the human who wants to be His image must be invisible too. All who educate for a visible ideal are pre-Christian. - SMI 144

JESUS

Jesus showed his divinity by taking on himself not earthly glory but ignominy and earthly suffering. Thus, instead of exploiting the hero worship of the masses, he emancipated them by sharing his divinity with them. - CF 108

THE JEWS

The Jews represent the end of human history before its actual end; without them pagan history would not only have had no goal, but would have gotten nowhere. The pagans represent the eternal new beginnings of history, and without them history would never have acquired any shape or form or beauty or fulfillment or attainment. God's Alpha was lived by the Gentiles, and God's Omega is embodied in the Jews. This antithesis brought pagans and Jews into a conflict of principle.... Wherever an old form is reluctant to go to its doom, like the Church in the fifteenth century, or like Czarism before 1914, it defends its own obsolete and dying institutions by persecuting the Jew, the eternal symbol of a life beyond any existing form of government. - OR 225-26

MIRACLES

What is a miracle? The natural law of a unique event. - VAU

THE NECESSARY

Nothing can stand in reality that isn't necessary. And God reveals himself only in the things necessary. Not in the things nice or the things you like. God is not interested in what you like at all. - UH6

ONE HISTORY

Man gives his acts an eternal, i.e. a "once-for-ever" meaning, by throwing his whole personality on the side of life that should now come forward, at each moment.... But he can select what should come forward only because one end of time, like a magnet, draws his heart at each step into the future. The uniqueness of the present derives from the uniqueness of the end. Hence only if history is one can our present-day acts have a once-for-ever meaning. People nowadays imagine that man and his history simply are one, but all the facts are against them. Unity is not given, not a natural fact, but a common task of some ninety-nine generations to date. - CF 71

THE "OTHER WORLD"

For us the difference between worldliness and otherworldliness is that between finite forms already created by the past and the infinite breath of the spirit which blows in upon us from the open future. The other world is in this world as man's destiny, man's meaning. - CF 125

PHILOSOPHY

You think that a Christian is an idealist. You even speak of philosophy—Christianity as a philosophy. It is an onslaught on philosophy! It laughs at philosophers. - UH6

PHILOSOPHY'S GOD

The Living God revealed by Jesus must be forever distinguished from the merely conceptual God of philosophers. Most atheists deny God because they look for Him in the wrong way. He is not an object but a person, and He has not a concept but a name. To approach Him as an object of theoretical discussion is to defeat the quest from the start. - CF 94

The Living God cannot be met on the level of natural reason because by definition He crosses our path in the midst of life, long after we have tried to think the world into a system. - CF 96

POLYTHEISM

Modern man is not so much godless as polytheistic, and therefore pagan. - CF 96

PRAYER

The idea that prayer is a private affair is erroneous. It is a worldwide institution as much as science, and it must check our other trends. The Jews checked these trends. They staked their whole existence on the faith that God, not man, is in process of creating Man. - JD 185

Prayer is speech that is spoken in the highest excitement because the act is extremely important and because, at the same time, we ourselves are relatively powerless. In such a crisis everything we say is either prayer or blasphemy. - JD 184

Human prayers anticipate the inevitable, and by anticipating they create a field of force for liberty. Liberty is nothing but the taking of death into our lives. - OR 513

RELIGION

Religion is never a private matter, neither of a sect, nor an association, nor of a circle. Religion is the power by which contact with the eternal asserts itself in everyday life and through which respect, order, obedience, future and meaning enter everyday life. - VZW 220

REVELATION

Revelation is orientation. - JN 21

SALVATION

Salvation always comes from where nobody expects it, from the depraved, from the impossible. It can only become salvation in that no human cunning can fathom it, in that it does not evolve within creation but freely enters creation as the Divine. - HK 285

SIN

Sin has become collective. The same doctor or manufacturer or mechanic or teacher who is so tame and good and overwrought that he has neither time nor opportunity to sin, belongs to one or more sinning groups. He belongs to a professional group, block, and lobby. They sin for him. - CF 30

THE SOUL

The human soul is the only specifically human element in man. - OR 724

The soul is that process by which generations are hinged, by which it is absolutely true that one generation suffers and the second generation harvests. - UH6

The soul is the carrier of the growing point, is the receptacle for the Holy Spirit, is still receiving new directions. You could put the problem very simply: anybody who has still an unknown future is, for this purpose, called a soul. - UH6

Predictability is all that is paid for in life. You see, we never get paid for our soul. - UH6

SPECULATIONS

Speculations over God and the world are almost always idle, the thoughts of idlers, spectators of the theater of life. "Is there a God?" "Has Man a soul?" "Why must we die?" "How many hairs has the Devil's Grandmother?" "When is the Day of Judgment?"—all these are idle questions, and one fool can ask more of them than a hundred wise men can answer. - VAU

THE SPIRIT

The third article of the Creed is the specifically Christian one: from now on the Holy Spirit makes man a partner in his own creation. In the beginning God had said, "Let us make man in our image" (Gen. 1:26). In this light, the Church Fathers interpreted human history as a process of making Man like God. They called it "anthropurgy": as metallurgy refines metal from its ore, anthropurgy wins the true stuff of Man out of his coarse physical substance. Christ, in the center of history, enables us to participate consciously in this man-making process and to study its laws. - CF 108

THE SUPERNATURAL

The supernatural should not be thought of as a magical force somehow competing with electricity or gravitation in the world of space, but as the power to transcend the past by stepping into an open future. - CF 123

THEOLOGY

Theology analyzes God as though he did not listen in at this very moment. As a result, the divine of neutral gender, as an inanimate object, is the theme of theology. Theology as the science of knowing God is at odds with faith in God, the unknowable. - OS 126

TIMING

Christ acquired a new faculty, the timing of the Spirit. He imparted to us this rightly timed spirit, this power not only to proclaim but also to obey these promptings in God's good time, neither too early nor too late. - IA 70

THE WORD

In the beginning there was neither mind nor matter. In the beginning was the Word. St. John was properly the first Christian theologian because he was overwhelmed by the spokenness of all meaningful happening. - CF 129

V. History

AMERICA

The sound of the axe is the natural philosophy of America. - OR 659

The sky of America is over Europe. The arts, the sciences, the Church, the Louvre, the Parliament, the pope, everything is situated in Europe. To this day America is a funny Egypt. The priests are in Europe and the laity is here. - UH6

AMERICA & RUSSIA

You consider yourselves a select group on this earth. There is no solidarity with the rest of the human race, except by charity. And the Russians, of course, have this great gospel that there is no salvation except for all. - COR

BEGINNING, MIDDLE & END

Meaningful history depends upon having one beginning, one middle, and one end. If our data are not oriented by single pillars of time in this way, history becomes a mere catalogue of changes, "1066 and all that." - CF 71

THE DYNAMITE OF REVOLUTION

The present time is bound to attempt an organization of future society by which the dynamite of revolution may be manipulated as persistently and consciously as contractors use real dynamite in building tunnels or roads. - OR 23

ECONOMIC BOUNDARIES

As we move toward wider and wider economic unification of the world, we must see to it that economic boundaries are not allowed to coincide with political ones, lest freedom vanish. - CF 40

EVOLUTION & REVOLUTION

Our revolutions must be raised to the square of their power before they can be understood in their deeper significance. They are not accidents of the kind which interest the reporter or the police, they are not sensational interruptions of an evolution which went on before and is resumed afterwards. They change the face of the earth. Evolution is based on revolution. It is sheer nonsense to put before us the choice between Evolution and Revolution. Revolution and Evolution are reciprocal ideas. - OR 466

THE FUTURE REVOLUTION

By its abolishing war, or changing it into civil war, the future revolution already presupposes the solidarity of mankind. As long as war was waged against unbelievers, pagans or Huns, civilized men could think of their foes as less than human. This is impossible now. Henceforth men are equals, and all wars are civil wars within one society. - OR 24

FOUNDERS

Any founder is a failure in the eyes of most of his contemporaries as compared to his immediately successful competitors. - CLF 66

THE FRENCH & RUSSIAN REVOLUTIONS

The French and Russian revolutions are results of the Christian era. They depend upon it, they complete it....The chief duty of any member of the Corpus Christi is to strengthen the other forms of humanity and thereby to assure the later co-ordination of the Russian antitheistic form with the rest of the Christian community. The economic unity of the world will probably offer an opportunity for co-operation between forces of life which are consciously Christian and others which suppress their Christian inheritance for the sake of restoring one single vital phase. - OR 716

GENERATIONS

Anything that is of more than one generation is interesting to history; anything that is limited to one generation is a freak. - UH4

The tree of everlasting life can grow only through successive generations of men reaching their hands to each other in one spirit across the ages. And *each generation has to act differently precisely in order to represent the same thing.* Only so can each become a full partner in the process of Making Man; only so can life be as authentic in the last age as in the first. - CF 130

GERMINAL ACTS

From germinal acts, not from action committees, authority results instead of tyranny, service instead of blueprints, fellowship instead of intellectual curiosity, creation instead of causation. - CF 193

GLOBAL SERVICE

Our peacemakers and planners must be supported by camps all over the globe, where youth, recruited from every town and village all over the globe, serves. This service must implement the global organization as the young must experience what the old are planning before the old can have any authority. - CF 238

THE GREAT SOCIETY

The Great Society, this speechless giant of the future, does not speak English (neither does it speak Russian)....The two world wars were the form of world revolution in which this new future reached into everybody's life; the nationalist and communist ideologies with their dreams of revolution were check-mated and are mere foam around the real transformation. The real transformation was made by the wars and it made the Great Society final. She is the heiress of State and Church. - CF 5

GREEKS, JEWS, TRIBES

We know what poetry is only from the Greeks. We know what prayer is only from the Jews. We know what a family is only from the tribes. - UH6

HISTORIANS

The historian is himself but the last act in the drama of an event. - AG 81

The historian is the physician of memory. It is his honor to heal wounds, genuine wounds. - OR 696

HISTORY & SCIENCE

History can never be a science. Science tells you how one thing follows from another. But history tells you how one thing emerges which has been denied by everything that went before it. History is the story of the unheard of things; science is the story of deducible things. History is a way of convincing you that new elements of life are created all the time. History is the story of creating, it is the knowledge of those events which must be known in themselves. In history nothing must be known but the unique, the unexpected, the unheard of, the surprising, the unbelievable. - UH4

ISRAEL

Israel built a temple, it is true, but they added that God did not dwell in it, as the gods of all other temples did: Israel voided the Temple. Israel circumcised her young men, it is true; but they did it to the child in the cradle, not to the initiate novice of the fertility orgies: Israel voided the rites. Israel wrote "poems," but she denied that she "wrote" them lest man-made "poems" became idols. She insisted that she was told and that she replied: Israel voided the arts. In these three acts she emptied the three great "speeches" of the heathen—the tribal, the templar, and the artistic—of their lure and spell and charm. - JD 181

LOVE & DEATH

The history of the human race is written on a single theme: How does love become stronger than death? The composition is recomposed in each generation by those whose love overcomes murdering or dying. So history becomes a great song, Augustine's *Carmen Humanum.* As often as the lines rhyme, love has once again become stronger than death. This rhyming, this connecting is men's function on earth. But that this is our function we have only known since the birth of Christ. - SOII 759

MYTH

Men of the Enlightenment believed that they themselves could live without myth. They ascribed to every time a *zeitgeist* to which one abandoned oneself without restraint. But *zeitgeist* is only a polite word for myth. For every attempt to identify one part of the world, a single country, a single century, with the whole world and the whole of time, is mythical. - FD 9

NATIONALISM

Nationalism makes every nation a chosen people in competition with all others. Messianism, originally limited to the Jews, later communicated to the heathen by the Church, is transferred by the European nationalism born in 1789 to the nations in general, which now enter upon a common race of messianic nationalism. - OR 236

NECESSITY

The Great Revolutions succeeded because they achieved something that was necessary....True statesmanship and true direction of one's own life are guided by instinct for the necessary. Arbitrariness is the death of men and nations. The category of necessity is beyond abstract good and evil—a category of the true future. - OR 719

THE NEW DEAL

The New Deal and the devaluation of the dollar are unthinkable without a preceding Bolshevik Revolution. The Great Revolutions are eccentric, they exaggerate, they are brutal and cruel. But the life of the rest of the world is regenerated by their outbreak. - OR 481

ONCE FOR ALL

An event which has not settled something once for all is of no importance to living men and women.... A preposterous attempt, a precursor, a stormy petrel, becomes valuable when we bring it into relation with the successful "once for all" achievement. The "once for all" principle works like a great sieve, sifting out quantities of superfluous traditions. - OR 75

PASSIONS

Our passions give life to the world. Our collective passions constitute the history of mankind. - OR 3

PAST & FUTURE

History is the acknowledgment that we stand facing two fronts: facing backward and facing forward. The man who thinks that he can stand looking into the past without at the same time looking into the future is wrong. - UH4

PEACE

Peace is not the sleep and the torpor of non-movement. Peace is not suspended animation. Peace is the victory over mere accident. Peace is the rhythm of a community which is still unfinished, still open to its true future. - CF 243

SALVATION

Human history is a process of the salvation of the world and the conversion of the pagans by the Word. - OR 235

STALINISM

The Communists cannot love, because for them no individual is permitted to resist the world plan. Yet the Russian people can love so strongly that they survive Stalinism. - SOI 189

THE THIRD MILLENNIUM

We enter today a third millennium. There's no doubt that by the year 2000 the world will have to have a religion, a different form of religion, or it will not exist. Mankind demands another group of leadership. You can't live by discoverers and inventors if you want to organize peace. - UH6

Paul, Saint-Simon, Paracelsus remained invisible to their contemporaries, and in the third millennium all continuation of life will depend on whether there will still be voluntary incognito. - SOII 33

THE THREE MILLENNIA

It is one story. The first thousand years made sure that everybody in this Western world would begin as a Christian. And the second thousand years built institutions, and preached to every son of women that they should reform the Church backward, and that they should discover God's creation, God's wide world. - UH4

Today we are living through the agonies of transition to the third epoch. We have yet to establish Man, the great singular of humanity, in one household, over the plurality of races, classes and age groups....The double concern of this epoch will be the revivification of all dead branches of the single human race, and the reinspiration of all mechanized portions of the single human life. - CF 115-16

TIMES

Periods, elements of times, are precisely elements by which we are transformed into a history. They are social creations. Times and spaces are "unnatural" circumstances of man. By their aid we enter the human family. - AG 101

THE TRIBES

What do we know of pre-historic tribes? What do the excavators find? They find tombs. Their way of reaching us over thousands of years is by burying the dead, by writing into the earth the story of their lives. The ancients knew that life begins when living persons set eyes on the dying, and the dying set eyes on the living. That is the strongest tie between the generations, just as the strongest tie between you and your wife is when you stand beside her in childbirth. We have no relation to the honor and the dignity of dying. Thus the ancients invented history by burying the dead. - UH4

TWOFOLD BEGINNING

Any important thing in history is founded twice, once by a stroke of genius, a second time by the labors of duty. - CLF 48

WAR

Wars are an expression of the "too late" of our thought and the helpless "too early" of our institutions. - CF 233

WAR & PEACE

Man is at war unless peace is made. Peace is not automatic but is always concluded. It has to be created; it is not natural. It is your mistake to think that peace is natural and war is unnatural. It is the other way around. Every time there has been a peace, it has been stated, it has been concluded. No step toward peace comes about by accident. It is an act of creation, a conscious effort, an effort of speech and inspiration. It is not ordinary but sublime to end a war....To be able to be in the shoes of the enemy is the only way to make peace. - CRO

THE WORLD REVOLUTIONS

The revolutions of mankind create new time-spans for our life on earth. They give man's soul a new relation between present, past and future; and by doing so they give us time to start our life on earth all over again, with a new rhythm and a new faith. - OR 14

What establishes the precedence of certain revolutions over the host of seditions and rebellions is the assumption of full responsibility for the whole past of mankind. - OR 524

Revolutions do nothing but readjust the equation between heart-power and social order. They come from the open and happen under the open sky. They bring about the Kingdom of God by force, and reach into the infinite in order to reform the finite. - OR 473

Revolutions do not create man; they build nurseries for his reproduction in a certain way and according to a certain type. - OR 467

All great revolutions re-create public law, public order, public spirit and public opinion; they all reform private customs, private manners and private feelings. They themselves must therefore live in a third dimension, beyond the reach of public law and private conviction. They live in the unprotected, unexplored and unorganized space which is hated by every civilization like hellfire itself—and which probably lies near hellfire. But it lies near heaven, too. Heaven and hell are the only words left to us for this character of openness and immediacy. - OR 468

VI. Thought & Science

ABSTRACT THINKING

Every abstract thinker tears love and time asunder. - VAU

THE ACADEMIC MODE

We learn before living; and after living we meditate. We learn much in preparation for the hour when it will be needed in earnest. The academic mode represents truth divorced from the moment of truth. - AG 32

Academic prejudices may be summed up as "obsession with space"—especially with external space and its corresponding ideal of "objectivity"—to the utter neglect of time. - IA 92

ART & SCIENCE

Art and science are supplementary, always. Science, with the torch of truth, emancipates the most simple soul. Art, with the awe of beauty, overawes the most sophisticated mind. - ROP 10

COMMUNISM

The Communist creed is like Islam: it demands acceptance of a complete intellectual system. It cannot help, therefore, separating men instead of uniting them. - MM 33

DEATH

The danger of death is the first cause of any knowledge about society. - SR 21

DEFINING

He who does not love defines. A defined god is my prisoner; he is a thing, for Aristotle the prime mover. - SOII 329

People who define on the first page analyze coagulated words. They start exactly at that point where the vital process ends. - SR 95

FAITH

Science is based on faith, on a very specific faith, perhaps, and the different sciences all anticipate different aspects of mankind's destiny. - CLF 68

GERMAN PHILOSOPHY

All German philosophy is but an attempt to remove the kingdom of heaven to a transcendental space and time which is inaccessible for mortals but which nevertheless stimulates us constantly to make a new (but hopeless) effort in the direction of the ideal. - OR 556

GNOSIS

Idealism and gnosis, in the guise of humanism, rule supreme in academia. Gnosis is simply the illusion that the retrieval of some truth in the mind makes superfluous the form in which this truth was first realized. - AG 18

THE GREEK MIND

The Greek mind is a method, a way of thinking, armchair philosophy, ivory tower. It does not include your real existence. The Greek mind is descriptive and universal, critical and factual. It is everything you want to be: objective, systematic, encyclopedic, philosophical. But it is not creative in the sense that it can tell one little child how to fold his hands and pray to God. The Greek mind thinks while sitting. The tribal mind, on the other hand, thinks while moving, in dance, in procession, and marching to war. The Greek mind insists on standing still, and the more static he can become, the better he can observe....The Greek way is a very passive experience. - UH4

HUMANISM

Humanism is an embellishment of life, but it is never a leader of it. It has no direction. Just embellishment. - UH5

IDEALISM

All this talk [about] materialism and idealism doesn't exist for a decent thinker. If I have to choose, I certainly am a materialist, because I believe in flesh and blood, in real people. I don't believe in ideals. - UH6

The everlasting idealist gives you the impression of a man who tries to prevent inspiration from ever coming true. - CLF 51

INSTITUTIONS

A new form of thought must be lived first before it may be externalized into endowed institutions. - CLF 43

INTELLECTUALISM

The intellect is a weather vane. It can serve any and every spirit or current in time. - AG 128

Our intellectuals are always above their problems, on the terra firma outside the oceans of risk. - CF 60

MENTALITY

Mentality is what is left of the soul when you abstract the crucifying experiences that bear fruit in more energetic and vital human relationships. Mentality knows nothing of jubilant joy and black despair, of yelling and cursing, moaning and groaning, shouting and dancing, and weeping and singing. Small wonder, then, that teaching and preaching become verbiage in the suburb. Its mentality emasculates the word. - CF 13

MONISM

Nature makes of mankind one observer, one mind. The monism of the scientific enlightenment lets men take the place which God took in monotheism. - OR 190

MYTH

A myth is a form of mental life which pretends to be deathless; its kernel is always a fixing of the mind on some transient thing which thereby is immortalized. Nothing on earth is good or forever. The myth pretends it to be. - CF 64

FROM PARMENIDES TO HEIDEGGER

From Homer to Parmenides the road was still open, the door to a common spirit of man was not closed. Solely after or with Parmenides did the metaphysical prison start in which subject and object, mind and body, nature and society, were forever split. From Parmenides to Heidegger a time-continuum exists, and whoever enters this maze called metaphysics or even philosophy, loses his membership in the pre-Greek humanity. - IA 77

PHILOSOPHY

Absolute idealism, absolute materialism, any *-ism* does not take into account the paradox that every man must have more than one philosophy during his life, and that a man's soul must be bigger than his mentality. All philosophies are partially true. Reality must be realized by more than one approach. The human soul is challenged today to see the relativity of all philosophical systems; hence, to survive any one of them. - SOL 22

But what else is the history of philosophy but the process of washing out the dye of Greece? - JD 142

PHYSICS

The last four centuries will, on the whole, have to be called a period in which physics and mathematics dominated the thought of Western Man. Even God and the law were proved by geometry. - CLF 53

PLATO

Communism, obviously, occupies a certain part of the spectrum of the human mind. Plato was a Communist, if ever there was one. So it isn't necessary to teach Communism. Just read Plato, and you will be instilled with this spirit. - UH4

THE PRIMARY QUESTIONS

The primary questions for an adult are not why or how, but when and where. - VAU

THE PRIME MOVER

The typical philosopher starts with the world of space and therefore never really gets outside it. God, for Aristotle, may be a logical necessity, but He can never be an experienced and telling reality because philosophy tries to be timeless. The prime mover knows nothing and provides nothing with regard to you or me. - CF 95

PROMISES

An education that does not give promises is not education. Claiming to give facts, and facts only, is a declaration of bankruptcy. Present day teaching is a series of farewell parties to life. - ESP 4

QUANTIFICATION

Each age has its specific political melody; ours is the music of numbers. - OR 70

REASON

We have a sense that urges us on toward Reason and Philosophy; this sense is curiosity. Without a sense for novelty no thinker can succeed or affect the life of the community. The self-indulgence of Reason is its predilection for the new....Reason is tickled by novelty. The nineteenth century changed the oldest truths into sensational news. - OR 248

RESPONDEO ETSI MUTABOR

We postwar thinkers are less concerned with the revealed character of the true God or the true character of nature than with the survival of a truly human society. In asking for a truly human society, we put the question of truth once more, but our specific endeavor is the living realization of truth in mankind. Truth is divine and has been divinely revealed—*credo ut intelligam.* Truth is pure and can be scientifically stated—*cogito ergo sum.* Truth is vital and must be socially represented—*respondeo etsi mutabor.* [I respond although I will be changed.] - OR 741

SCIENCE

In a sense, all science is nearly speechless; it is a whisper between experts. Only when taught, only when facing a new generation, does science recover speech. - CF 229

Science is a campaign of mankind, balancing in any given moment, past experience, present speculation, and future experimentation, in a unique concoction of scepticism, faith, doubt, and expectation. - CLF 1

SOCIOLOGY

Sociology is the economy of salvation and was founded by St. Augustine. - AG 96

SPEAK TO THE EAGLE!

You either speak to the eagle, and he lives. Or you speak of the eagle, and he will become taxidermy. And we have taxidermic wildlife today. That's all we have. And all the sciences we have created of the living are a mummification. We have made mummies of the whole universe. - COR

TEACHING

Surely all education is based on our ability to renounce preconceived images of man. - AG 138

The truth of teaching is proven by its ability to inspire even those furthest removed from it. - AG 134

The more vital anything is that is taught, the more chance there will be of misunderstanding. Two plus two equals four offers less opportunity for misunderstanding than the statement, "Europe has committed suicide." For that very reason, the latter is much more important. - AG 119

When we look at teaching from the end of man, from the regeneration of the universal order, we shall treat the student as the founder of centuries. - ESP 4

TECHNOLOGY

Every technological advance shortens time, widens space, and destroys a familiar living group. - PS 53

THINKING VERSUS SPEAKING

The 19th century asked: what does the thinker do to the things he thinks about? We ask: what happens to the speaker as the result of his speaking? - JN 118

THOUGHT

Thought is an aggregate condition of speech, similar to the relation of steam to ice and water. - JN 227

TRANSLATION

The greatness of the human being is that he can translate into his own language. Men wish to admire only that which they cannot translate themselves. If you do that, you will be the unhappiest of persons. The simplest truths, when translated, are the most profound. - CRO

To think means to translate from one language into another better language. - SR 71

THE UNIVERSITY

If the university does not reform, it cannot perform. The university is the future of the country dealt with beforehand. - GU 20

Bibliographies

I. Books by Eugen Rosenstock-Huessy

The letter reference codes in front of the titles on the following pages will enable the reader to identify the sources quoted in this book.

This bibliography lists all Rosenstock-Huessy's major books in English and German (32 titles). For a comprehensive listing, including booklets and pamphlets (37 works) as well as articles (388 works), see bibliography by Lise van der Molen published in *Speech and Society* by George Morgan (see section III below).

Books listed with a price (16 titles) are currently (1988) available from Argo Books at those prices (Box 710, Norwich, VT 05055). Please mail check and add 10% for postage and handling. A 16-page catalog describing the books is available on request. To order books in Europe, write to the following address for details on availability and method of payment: Argo Books, Pijperstraat 20, Heemskerk, Netherlands.

AK *Das Alter der Kirche.* (With Joseph Wittig.) Berlin: Lambert Schneider, 1927-28. 3 Vols., 1,250 pp.

AG *Der Atem des Geistes.* Frankfurt: Verlag der Frankfurter Hefte, 1951. 293 pp.

CF *The Christian Future.* Harper, 1966. 306 pp., paperback, $6.95 from ARGO. First published by Scribner's, 1946. Also in German as *Des Christen Zukunft.* Munich: Kaiser, 1955. Current German edition - Mors: Brendow Verlag, 1985.

ER *Die Europäischen Revolutionen und der Charakter der Nationen.* Kohlhammer, 1951, 584 pp.; revised edition, 1961. These two editions are revisions of the original - Jena: Eugen Diedrichs, 1931. 554 pp.

FD *Frankreich-Deutschland.* Berlin: Vogt, 1957. 106 pp.

FL *The Fruit of Lips.* Pickwick, 1978. 144 pp., paperback, $5.25 from ARGO.

GU *Das Geheimnis der Universität.* Kohlhammer, 1958. 320 pp.

HF *Herzogsgewalt und Friedensschutz.* Breslau: M. & H. Marcus, 1910. 205 pp. Reprinted, Aalen: Scientia Verlag, 1969.

HW *Heilkraft und Wahrheit*. Stuttgart: Evangelisches Verlagswerk, 1952. 215 pp.

HK *Die Hochzeit des Kriegs und der Revolution*. Würzburg: Patmos, 1920. 306 pp.

IA *I Am an Impure Thinker*. ARGO, 1970. 206 pp., hardbound, $10.00; paperback, $6.95.

IK *Im Kampf um die Erwachsenenbildung*. (With Werner Picht.) Leipzig: Quelle & Meyer, 1926. 240 pp.

IR *Industrierecht*. Berlin: H. Sack, 1926. 183 pp.

JN *Ja und Nein*. Heidelberg: Lambert Schneider, 1968. 184 pp.

JD *Judaism Despite Christianity*. University of Alabama Press, 1969. 198 pp., hardbound, $12.95; paperback by Schocken, 1971, $6.50 from ARGO.

KS *Königshaus und Stämme*. Leipzig: Felix Meiner, 1914. Reprint ed., Aalen: Scientia, 1965. 416 pp.

ML *Magna Carta Latina*. (With Ford Lewis Battles.) Pickwick, 1975. 296 pp., paperback, $6.50 from ARGO.

MM *The Multiformity of Man*. ARGO, 1973. 78 pp., paperback, $3.50. First book edition was Norwich, Vt.: Beachhead, 1949; published as pamphlet 1936. Also in German as *Der unbezahlbare Mensch*. Berlin: Vogt, 1955 and Herder, 1964.

OF *Östfalens Rechtsliteratur unter Friedrich II.* Weimar: Hermann Böhlaus Nachfolger, 1912. 147 pp.

OS *The Origin of Speech*. ARGO, 1981. 160 pp., paperback, $6.50.

OR *Out of Revolution*. ARGO, 1969. 795 pp., paperback, $12.00. First published - William Morrow, 1938.

PS *Planetary Service*. ARGO, 1978. 144 pp., paperback, $6.00. In German as *Dienst auf dem Planeten*. Kohlhammer, 1965.

RP *Rosenstock-Huessy Papers, Vol. I.* ARGO, 1981. 245 pp., paperback, $18.00. (A collection of nine typed manuscripts. Listed with asterisks in section II below.)

SOI *Soziologie Bd. I. Die Übermacht der Raüme.* Kohlhammer, 1956. 335 pp. This is a substantially revised version of the 1925 edition - Berlin: Walter de Gruyter. 264 pp.

SOII *Soziologie Bd. II. Die Vollzahl der Zeiten.* Kohlhammer, 1958. 774 pp.

SR *Speech and Reality.* With introduction by Clinton C. Gardner. ARGO, 1970. 201 pp., paperback, $6.95.

SMI *Die Sprache des Menschengeschlechts. Bd. I.* Heidelberg: Lambert Schneider, 1963. 810 pp.

SMII *Die Sprache des Menschengeschlechts. Bd. II.* Heidelberg: Lambert Schneider, 1964. 904 pp.

WA *Werkstattaussiedlung.* Berlin: J. Springer, 1922. 286 pp.

ZW *Zurück in das Wagnis der Sprache.* Berlin: Vogt, 1957. 81 pp.

II. Articles, Papers & Tapes

Listed below are articles, papers and tape recordings by Eugen Rosenstock-Huessy from which selections have been made for this book. Asterisks indicate the nine papers included in *Rosenstock-Huessy Papers, Vol. I,* listed above. Please write to Argo Books for a complete listing of recorded lectures (over 30 listings) as well as information on prices and availability of cassette copies and typed transcriptions.

The Rosenstock-Huessy Fund has recently undertaken to recopy and transcribe most of Rosenstock-Huessy's recorded lectures. Many will thus become available as typed and bound transcriptions.

ARC - "The Artist and His Community" (1940).

CIR - "The Circulation of Thought." Dartmouth College, Feb.-May 1954 (Philosophy 10). 26 lectures on tapes.

CLF - "A Classic and a Founder" (1937).*

COR - "Comparative Religion." Dartmouth College, Sept.-Dec. 1954 (Religion 40). 25 lectures on tapes.

CRO - "The Cross of Reality." Dartmouth College, Oct. 1953-Jan. 1954 (Philosophy 9). 23 lectures on tapes.

ESP - "Education, The Strategy of Peace" (undated), Dartmouth Library.

FEW - "Friedensbedingungen einer Weltwirtschaft," *Offene Welt,* Jan.-Feb. 1959.

FWL - "The Future Way of Life" (1942).*

GNF - "The Generations of the Faith" (1961).*

INV - *Industrievolk.* Frankfurt: Carolus-Druckerei, 1924. 55 pp.

LAL - "Language, Logic, Literature" (1939).

LTT - "Liturgical Thinking" (1949).*

MMT - "Man Must Teach" (about 1940).*

MBS - "The Metabolism of Science" (about 1945).*

OUG - "Our Urban Goggles" (1948).*

PEM - "Pentecost and Mission," Hartford Seminary Foundation Bulletin (Winter 1954/1955), pp. 17-25.

PSI - "Partner und Stämme der Industrie," *Neues Abendland* 6, June 1953.

ROP - "The Release of Poetry" (about 1940).

SBA - "The Science of Bodies and The Appeal to Somebody" (1938).*

SOL - "Soldiers in the Larger Sense" (undated).

TBD - "Time Bettering Days" (1954).*

TIH - "Time and Historicity of Man," in Sidney and Beatrice Rome, eds., *Philosophical Interrogations* (New York: Holt, Rinehart and Winston, 1964), pp 31-35.

UH4 - "Universal History." Dartmouth College, Feb.-May 1954 (Philosophy 58). 23 lectures on tapes.

UH6 - "Universal History." Dartmouth College, April-June, 1956 (Philosophy 58). Partial: 10 lectures on tapes.

VAU - These letters indicate a Rosenstock-Huessy quotation selected by W. H. Auden for *The Viking Book of Aphorisms* (Viking, 1962). These quotations have been included even though their original book reference could not be located.

VZW - "Das Volk zwischen Himmel und Erde," *Das evangelische Deutschland*, July 3, 1932.

III. Books about Eugen Rosenstock-Huessy

M. Darrol Bryant and Hans R. Huessy, eds., *Eugen Rosenstock-Huessy: Studies in His Life and Thought*. Lewiston, N.Y.: The Edwin Mellen Press, 1986. 270 pp., hardbound, $29.00 from ARGO.

Clinton C. Gardner, *Letters to The Third Millennium: An Experiment in East-West Communication*. ARGO, 1981. 272 pp., hardbound, $12.95; paperback, $7.95.

Clinton C. Gardner, ed., *Life Lines: Quotations from the Work of Eugen Rosenstock-Huessy*. With bibliography and biography. ARGO, 1988. 96 pp., paperback, $5.95.

George Allen Morgan, *Speech and Society: The Christian Linguistic Social Philosophy of Eugen Rosenstock-Huessy*. Comprehensive bibliography by Lise van der Molen. University of Florida Press, 1987. 220 pp., hardbound, $24.95 from ARGO.

Jack J. Preiss, *Camp William James*. ARGO, 1978. 272 pp., hardbound, $12.00; paperback, $7.00.

Harold Stahmer, *"Speak That I May See Thee!": The Religious Significance of Language*. Macmillan, 1968. 304 pp. (Currently out of print.)

Eugen Rosenstock-Huessy at 65 in his study at Four Wells, his Vermont home, 1953

Biography of Eugen Rosenstock-Huessy

Eugen Rosenstock-Huessy was born in Berlin, Germany in 1888, the son of a Jewish banker. After receiving his doctorate in law and philosophy from Heidelberg University, he taught law at Leipzig University from 1912 to 1914. In the First World War he was an officer at the front near Verdun.

During the war he and his friend Franz Rosenzweig conducted an extended correspondence on Judaism and Christianity. Rosenstock-Huessy, who had embraced Christianity as a young man, had almost convinced his friend Rosenzweig to do the same. Their letters, first published in the 1920s, have been widely commented on as a classic contemporary confrontation between Christian and Jew.

In 1914 he married Margrit Huessy and added his wife's surname to his own, in the Swiss custom. After the war he did not return to the university but instead went to work for Daimler-Benz at their Stuttgart automobile manufacturing plant. There, in 1919-21, he founded and edited the first factory magazine in Germany. In 1921-22 he founded and headed The Academy of Labor at Frankfurt, a pioneering effort in adult education. Later, in 1929, he was elected vice-chairman of the World Association for Adult Education.

He returned to university life in 1923, as professor of law at the University of Breslau. In 1924 he published *Angewandte Seelenkunde (An Applied Science of the Soul),* his first formulation of a proposed method for the social sciences, a method based on speech. This was followed in 1925 by an elaborated formulation of the method in a book entitled *Soziologie.* When his Roman Catholic friend Joseph Wittig was excommunicated, he wrote with him a book on church history, *Das Alter der Kirche (The Age of the Church),* and published it in 1928.

While at Breslau, in 1928-30, he organized voluntary work service camps which brought together workers, farmers and students in work together on the land. This, and his subsequent similar activities in the United States, have been described as forerunners of the United States Peace Corps.

In 1931 he published a major historical work, *Die Europäischen Revolutionen (The European Revolutions),* a book which established his reputation in Europe. A completely rewritten version of this book was published in the United States in 1938 as *Out of Revolution.*

Immediately after Hitler came to power in 1933, he voluntarily left Germany and went to the United States. After teaching three years at Harvard, he joined the faculty at Dartmouth College, where he taught as professor of social philosophy until his retirement in 1957.

With the backing of President Franklin Roosevelt, in 1940 he organized an experimental camp within the Civilian Conservation Corps. Camp William James in Tunbridge, Vermont was experimental in that it was to train leaders for a possible development of the CCC into a service that would accept volunteers from all walks of life, not simply young men in need of work.

He continued to write throughout the period 1940 to 1960, publishing *The Christian Future* in 1945 and a much-expanded *Soziologie* in two volumes in 1956-58. The second volume is a universal history of man interpreted in the spirit of the new method which is the subject of volume one. In 1963 he published a major work on speech and the relation of speech to his method, *Die Sprache des Menschengeschlechts (The Speech of Mankind).* During the 1950s he lectured at the German universities of Göttingen, Cologne and Münster. In the 1960s he lectured in the United States at Columbia University, New York, the University of California at Santa Cruz, and at other California campuses.

From 1937 until his death in 1973 he made his home in Norwich, Vermont.